Record-Breaking Comprehension
Year 3

Teacher's Book
Alison Milford

Published by
RISING★STARS
in association with
GUINNESS
WORLD
RECORDS

Rising Stars UK Ltd.
7 Hatchers Mews, Bermondsey Street, London, SE1 3GS
www.risingstars-uk.com

Published 2013
Reprinted 2013, 2014 (twice), 2015
All underlying records data © Guinness World Records Ltd.
Published in association with Guinness World Records.

Author: Alison Milford
Text design: Burville-Riley Partnership/Words & Pictures Ltd
Typesetting: Words & Pictures Ltd
Cover design: Burville-Riley Partnership
Publisher: Becca Law
Project manager: Tracey Cowell
Editor: Jennie Clifford

Photo acknowledgements
Page 9: © Michael Caven/iStockphoto; **page 11**: © Nastco/iStockphoto; **page 13**: Ivana Boskov/iStockphoto; **page 17**: Linearcurves/iStockphoto; **page 21**: wittyn11/iStockphoto; **page 23**: © Brown Dog Studios/iStockphoto; **page 27**: Jamie Carroll, LLC/iStockphoto; **page 33**: Bortonia/iStockphoto, Draco77/iStockphoto, Karlov Sergey/iStockphoto; **page 35**: 4x6/iStockphoto; **page 39**: HKPNC/iStockphoto; **page 41**: pixitive/iStockphoto; **page 43**: Kathryn8/iStockphoto; **page 47**: Jerrzone/iStockphoto; **page 49**: vadimmmus/iStockphoto; **page 51**: The_guitar_mann/iStockphoto; **page 55**: artbyjulie/iStockphoto.
Rising Stars is grateful to Guinness World Records for supplying all of the record-related pictures in the book.

British Library Cataloguing in Publication Data.
A CIP record for this book is available from the British Library.

ISBN: 978-0-85769-567-3

Printed by Ashford Colour Press

CONTENTS

GUINNESS WORLD RECORDS

HOW TO USE THIS BOOK

Record-Breaking Comprehension is a brand new resource that uses the appeal of Guinness World Records to engage pupils in reading comprehension texts.

The records are described via a range of fiction and non-fiction text types, including newspaper reports, instructional web pages, blog entries and letters. The grid on pages 6–7 summarises the text types covered.

This Teacher's Book provides:

- answers to the questions, plus guidance on AFs and question types covered;

- support and research pointers for the Beyond the Record activities;

- photocopiable activities for writing, speaking and listening, linked to each record.

GUINNESS WORLD RECORDS — RECORD-BREAKING COMPREHENSION – YEAR 3

MOST PEOPLE READING ALOUD SIMULTANEOUSLY – SINGLE LOCATION

This email-style recount text is written from the perspective of a child who helped to break the Guinness World Record for most people reading aloud simultaneously, in Turkey.

Text type:	recount/information
AFs covered:	AF2, AF3, AF5, AF6
Specialist vocabulary:	simultaneously, stadium, volunteer, ticket, chapter, aloud

ON YOUR MARKS

a. 23,822 people broke the world record. *Literal AF2*
b. You can tell it is an email by the name and subject layout at the top. *Deduction AF3, AF4*
c. *Personal opinion AF2, AF3*

GET SET

a. The book Habib read from was called *Les Misérables*. *Literal AF2*
b. It sounded 'awesome' because thousands of people were reading the book aloud at the same time. *Inference AF3, AF5, AF6*
c. It was 'incredible news' because the event involved so many people and because Habib had become a Guinness World Record holder. *Deduction AF3, AF6*

GO FOR GOLD!

a. Habib was given a ticket when he arrived at the stadium. *Literal AF2*
b. Habib found it spooky because a stadium full of people would normally be very loud but it was completely silent. *Inference AF3, AF5*
c. *Personal opinion AF2, AF3, AF6*

BEYOND THE RECORD

Research the Malatya Inönü Stadium on the internet. Produce a fact sheet about it. Find out about three other stadiums around the world and add the information to your fact sheet.

Background research, reading and discussion to help the children to prepare

- Explain that the word *stadium* means a venue for large events such as sports events and concerts. Discuss who would want to read a fact sheet on stadiums. What information would they expect?
- As a class, search Wikipedia (en.wikipedia.org/) for Malatya Inönü Stadium.
- Guide children to websites with information on world stadiums: www.worldstadiums.com/; en.wikipedia.org/wiki/List_of_stadiums_by_capacity; www.topendsports.com/events/summer/stadiums.htm.

Recording their ideas

- What style of fact sheet are they going to produce: paragraphs with sub-headings, headings with simple bulleted facts? Will they use any images?

- Encourage the children to think about how they record the information they find out from websites, e.g. using sticky notes, drawing a rough layout of a fact sheet and writing in notes.

Ideas may include: location, capacity, the number of seats, when it was built, types of events, famous events, design.

LANGUAGE ACTIVITY WORKSHEET

- This worksheet allows the children to practise proofreading a text for commonly misspelled words. Provide the children with the worksheet and explain that 10 of the words have been misspelled. It is their task to proofread the text to locate and underline the 10 mistakes.
- They must then write out the correct spellings in the spelling box under the text. Allow access to dictionaries and word banks to help them. When the children have found and corrected the mistakes they could self-mark or mark another's work, using the text from the Pupil Book.

Answers: knews (news), peple (people), family (family), uther (other), arrivd (arrived), realy (really), hole (whole), red (read), droped (dropped), wold (world)

Reading comprehension questions

The reading comprehension questions in the Pupil Book are split into three differentiated sections: On your marks, Get set and Go for gold! The questions within each section become increasingly more challenging. For Years 3 and 4, there are three questions in each section; this increases to four questions per section for Years 5 and 6. You may wish to ask different groups of children to answer a particular set, or sets, of questions, depending on their ability.

The questions cover a range of AFs and question types (literal, inference, deduction and personal opinion), details of which can be found with the answers. A summary of coverage can be found on the grid on pages 6–7.

Language activity worksheets

Each of the photocopiable activity worksheets focuses on different language features and skills that children need to develop within the year group, and includes grammar, spelling and punctuation activities.

There are suggestions for how to introduce each worksheet, as well as teaching prompts. A summary of the coverage for the worksheets can be found in the grid on pages 6–7.

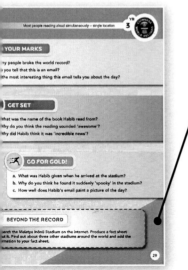

Beyond the record

These follow-up activities can be used with any child, regardless of their level and progress through the reading comprehension questions. Many of the activities involve children researching more about the record and presenting their findings.

Each activity is accompanied by structured teacher's notes, including web references where appropriate. The activities can be used both for class work and homework.

CONTENT SUMMARY GRID

Record title	Text type	AF coverage	Worksheet focus
Deepest underwater postbox	Postcards: recount	AF2, AF3	Homophones
Largest seashell mosaic	Newsletter: recount/explanation	AF2, AF3, AF5	Ordering instructions
Oldest wing walker	Book: non-chronological report/explanation	AF2, AF3, AF4, AF5	Verbs and adjectives
Largest Sinosauropteryx fossil	Poster: persuasion	AF2, AF3, AF5, AF6	Proofreading/dictionary use
Largest mask	Travel guide: non-chronological report/recount	AF2, AF3	Inverted commas for speech
Narrowest street	Travel magazine: non-chronological report	AF2, AF3, AF5	Suffixes
Most spoons balanced on the face	TV script: recount/instructions	AF2, AF3, AF4, AF6	Suffixes, adjectives and adverbs
Most consecutive haircuts by a team in eight hours	Blog: recount	AF2, AF3, AF6	Punctuation: full stops, exclamations and questions
Heaviest car balanced on the head	Formal letter	AF2, AF3, AF4, AF5	The *ai* sound
Largest orchestra playing on recycled materials	Poster: persuasion	AF2, AF3, AF4, AF5, AF6	The verb *to have*
Most people reading aloud simultaneously – single location	Email: recount	AF2, AF3, AF5, AF6	Proofreading/dictionary use
Tallest sunflower	Book: explanation/non-chronological report	AF2, AF3, AF4, AF6	Adjectives/using a thesaurus
Longest tongue	Magazine article: explanation	AF2, AF3	Alliteration
Largest human wheelbarrow race	TV script: recount	AF2, AF3, AF4	Solutions for longer spellings

Record title	Text type	AF coverage	Worksheet focus
Most people skipping – single venue	Newsletter: persuasion/recount	AF2, AF3, AF4, AF6	Time adverbs
Most forward rolls in one hour – individual	Blog: biography	AF2, AF3, AF4, AF5	Prefixes
Fastest marathon carrying a 60-lb pack	Website: biography	AF2, AF3, AF5	Prepositions
Most leaves on a clover stem	Book: recount	AF2, AF3	Collective nouns
Farthest ear sling-shot	Magazine article: explanation/recount	AF2, AF3, AF4, AF5	Determiners *a* and *an*
Fastest crossing of the Sahara Desert by bicycle	Blog: recount	AF2, AF3	Time and cause conjunctions
Longest journey by powered paraglider	Book: recount	AF2, AF3, AF5, AF6	Proper nouns
Largest collection of Pooh and Friends memorabilia	Magazine article: recount	AF2, AF3, AF5	Paragraphs
Largest museum devoted to dinosaurs	Museum leaflet: persuasion	AF2, AF3, AF5	Sub-headings to organise text
Most steps climbed by bicycle	Magazine article: non-chronological report/recount	AF2, AF3, AF5, AF6	Prefixes

DEEPEST UNDERWATER POSTBOX

These postcard-style recount texts are written from the perspective of a holidaymaker visiting Susami Bay in Japan. He writes about finding an underwater postbox, which holds the Guinness World Record for the deepest underwater postbox.

Text type:	recount
AFs covered:	AF2, AF3
Specialist vocabulary:	underwater, postcard, waterproof, deepest, Susami Bay, Japan

ANSWERS

ON YOUR MARKS

a. The world's deepest underwater postbox is in Susami Bay, Wakayama-Ken in Japan. *Literal AF2*
b. Dan was surprised because you don't usually see a postbox at the bottom of the sea. *Inference AF3*
c. Dan would need a waterproof postcard because a normal postcard would become soggy. *Inference AF3*

GET SET

a. The world's deepest underwater postbox became a record holder on 23 April 1999. *Literal AF2*
b. Dan thought the postbox was sunken treasure because treasure is more likely to be found underwater than a postbox. *Inference AF3*
c. Dan is enjoying his holiday. He is having fun exploring the underwater world. *Deduction AF3*

GO FOR GOLD!

a. Up to 200 postcards can be posted in the underwater postbox on a busy day. *Literal AF2*
b. The postman needs a plastic key as a metal key would become rusty from the water. *Inference AF3*
c. *Personal opinion AF3*

BEYOND THE RECORD

Use two sources of information to find out more about unusual postboxes in the world. Where are they? Who uses them? Who picks up the post? Use the information to create a fact sheet and remember to record where you found the information.

Background research, reading and discussion to help the children to prepare

- As a class, search online for images of unusual postboxes around the world. You could focus on different categories such as size (largest, tallest, smallest), location (deepest underground, highest, desert, outback, arctic, rainforest) or design.
- Guide the children to relevant websites for their research, such as www.poldark-mine.co.uk, www.postalheritage.org.uk and the Wikipedia entry for 'Post box' at en.wikipedia.org/wiki/Post_box.

Recording their ideas

- Allow the children to choose their own method of making notes. Remind them to record where they found their information.
- Encourage the children to decide how they are going to set out their fact sheets, e.g. as printed images with written captions, a list of information with sub-headings and diagrams, a table with answers to set questions. Will their fact sheets be written or completed on the computer?

Feedback: Encourage the children to share their fact sheets. Are the fact sheets clear and do they give the correct information?

LANGUAGE ACTIVITY WORKSHEET

- Remind the children what a homophone is. Choose a couple of examples from Year 2 such as *sea/see*, *bare/bear* and *blue/blew*. Ask the children to give you sentence examples for each word and write them down for the children to see.
- Ask the children to look at the top of the worksheet and read out the homophone examples. Encourage the children to underline the correct homophones in the two postcards. Encourage them to use dictionaries if they are not sure of the correct word to choose.
- Once they have underlined the homophones, ask the children to check to see if they have got the right answers. Discuss which ones they found hard and talk about strategies that could help them remember the different spellings and meanings, e.g. visual patterns, association to something, etc.

Answers: Dear, great, plane, mist, rain, sun, beach, bury, piece, which, medal, not, wait, here.

OFFICIALLY AMAZING

POSTING HOMOPHONES

Homophones are words that sound the same but are spelled differently.
I am going to *mail* my postcard.
A *male* sheep is called a ram.

Underline the correct homophones in the postcards.

(Deer/Dear) Joe

We're having a (grate/great) time in Spain. When we got off the (plane/plain) this morning, there was lots of (mist/missed) and (rein/rain) but the (sun/son) soon came out. Going to the (beach/beech) tomorrow.

Jake

Joe Black

29 Fillsbury Avenue

Shorting

ST26 2UR

ENGLAND

Hi Joe

Had an amazing day! As I was trying to (berry/bury) Chloe's feet in the sand, I saw a (piece/peace) of metal (which/witch) looked like a small (medal/meddle). It did (not/knot) have a name on it so Dad gave it to the police.

Can't (weight/wait) for tomorrow's adventure!

Wish you were (here/hear).

Jake

Joe Black

29 Fillsbury Avenue

Shorting

ST26 2UR

ENGLAND

LARGEST SEASHELL MOSAIC

This newsletter recount is about the Dubai Police Force who, on 17 January 2010, broke the Guinness World Record for the largest seashell mosaic.

Text type:	recount/explanation
AFs covered:	**AF2, AF3, AF5**
Specialist vocabulary:	mosaic, seashell, collect, dhow, officer, beach

ANSWERS

ON YOUR MARKS

a. **It took 130 people to make the seashell mosaic.** *Literal AF2*
b. **The seashells had to be sorted so that good (unbroken) shells could be used for the mosaic.** *Inference AF3*
c. *Personal opinion AF3*

GET SET

a. **59,835 seashells were used in the mosaic.** *Literal AF2*
b. **The Dubai Police Force admire and like the ruler of Dubai because they made the mosaic for his fourth year as ruler.** *Inference AF3*
c. **It took a long time to make the mosaic because of all the stages involved. It had to be designed, and seashells had to be collected, sorted, laid out and stuck down.** *Deduction AF3*

GO FOR GOLD!

a. **A 'dhow' is a boat.** *Literal AF2*
b. **'Unveiled' means that the mosaic is shown after it has been covered up or hidden.** *Inference AF3, AF5*
c. **The Dubai Police Force, who made the mosaic, chose part of their police logo. The logo includes a dhow, which shows the importance of the sea to the people of Dubai.** *Deduction AF3*

BEYOND THE RECORD

Read the text again and make notes on the different stages of how the seashell mosaic was made. Choose a way to present this information to others – for example, on a flow chart, a poster with diagrams and captions, or a presentation on a computer.

Background research, reading and discussion to help the children to prepare

• Find different examples of instructional texts (such as recipes or craft activities) that explain how to make something. Discuss the similarities of each text such as a logical sequence, time connectives, lists, etc.

• Use one of the example texts to demonstrate how to scan a text to make notes. Discuss the different ways the children could make notes, e.g. using a highlighter pen, writing notes in the margin or underlining text.

Recording their ideas

• Encourage the children to choose their own way of making notes from the text. Discuss whether their chosen style of note taking helps them or if another way would work better.

• Ask children to decide what type of presentation they will use to show how the mosaic is created. What features will it include: a logical sequence, list of materials, connectives, numbered lists?

Feedback: Encourage the children to share their set of instructions. Discuss what makes instructions easy to follow and how children could improve their instructions.

LANGUAGE ACTIVITY WORKSHEET

• This worksheet looks at paragraph order and how instructional steps are ordered.

• After the children have decided on the correct order of the paragraphs, encourage them to read out the text. Does it make sense? Why is it important to have different sections/paragraphs? Why do they need to be in the right order?

Answers: The order of the steps is: 4, 6, 1, 5, 3, 2.

OFFICIALLY AMAZING

THE SHELL SHUFFLE

The text below gives instructions on how to make shell animals, but the paragraphs are in the wrong order.

Cut out each paragraph and stick them on a piece of paper in the correct order. Do they make sense?

Then, when you get home, wash them gently in clean water to get rid of the sand and any dirt.

Finally, decorate the shell models so they look like animals.

After that, you need to glue the shells gently into place and then leave them to dry.

Making model animals out of shells is easy and fun. This is how you do it.

Next, set out the shells. Use large flat shells for heads and bodies and smaller shells for parts such as legs and ears.

First, you need to go to the beach to collect unbroken shells of different colours, shapes and sizes.

OLDEST WING WALKER

This information text is about Thomas Lackey, who, on 30 May 2012, broke the Guinness World Record for the oldest wing walker. It also explains how and when wing walking started and who was involved.

Text type:	non-chronological report/explanation
AFs covered:	AF2, AF3, AF4, AF5
Specialist vocabulary:	wing, walking, stunt, circus, dangerous, daring, oldest, flying, performing

ANSWERS

ON YOUR MARKS

a. The world's oldest wing walker is Thomas Lackey. *Literal AF2*
b. Many wing walkers died because they did dangerous stunts on the wings of flying planes. *Inference AF3*
c. *Personal opinion AF3*

GET SET

a. Thomas Lackey broke the record on 30 May 2012. *Literal AF2*
b. Ormer Locklear first climbed onto wings of flying planes to fix them. He continued to wing walk because he enjoyed the experience. *Literal AF2, inference AF3*
c. Wing walkers now have to be tied to a plane as it is safer and makes it less likely that they will fall off. *Deduction AF3*

GO FOR GOLD!

a. Wing walkers used to perform the following stunts: handstands, playing tennis, dancing or moving from one plane to another (accept any three of these). *Literal AF2*
b. 'Daring' can mean brave, risky, adventurous or reckless. *Inference AF3, AF5*
c. Possible answers include scary, exhilarating, exciting, wonderful, terrifying. *Personal opinion AF2, AF5*

BEYOND THE RECORD

Use the internet to find out more about wing walking as a hobby. Plan the content for a wing-walking web page. Include information about the:
- wing-walking teachers
- pilots
- planes
- cost
- stunts.

Background research, reading and discussion to help the children to prepare
- Discuss with the children how they can gather information about wing-walking experiences to help them plan their web page.
- Guide the children to look at websites dedicated to wing walking, such as www.aerosuperbatics.com and let them research through the content for ideas.

Recording their ideas
- Encourage the children to make a list of important things to include on the page, e.g. where you can wing walk, directions, cost, who helps you, what you need to take, etc.
- Ask the children to think about how they would present their web page, e.g. using a presentation package, poster, sketches.

Feedback: Encourage the children to ask for feedback on their plan. Does it give clear, concise information? Does it make the reader want to wing walk? If not, what needs to be added?

LANGUAGE ACTIVITY WORKSHEET

- Use the worksheet to consolidate how different verbs and adjectives can be used in connection with wing walking or flying. They could be taken from the comprehension text, children's answers to Go for gold! c., or the children could list other verbs and adjectives.
- Encourage the children to use the third flag to think of other sky sports, such as gliding, hang-gliding and parachuting.
- The fourth flag could be used for vocabulary extension, such as a word bank, research words, or phrases such as 'ground speed'.
- Discuss children's choices.

FLYING THE FLAG

How many words can you think of that are linked to wing walking or flying?
Write at least three words in each flag.

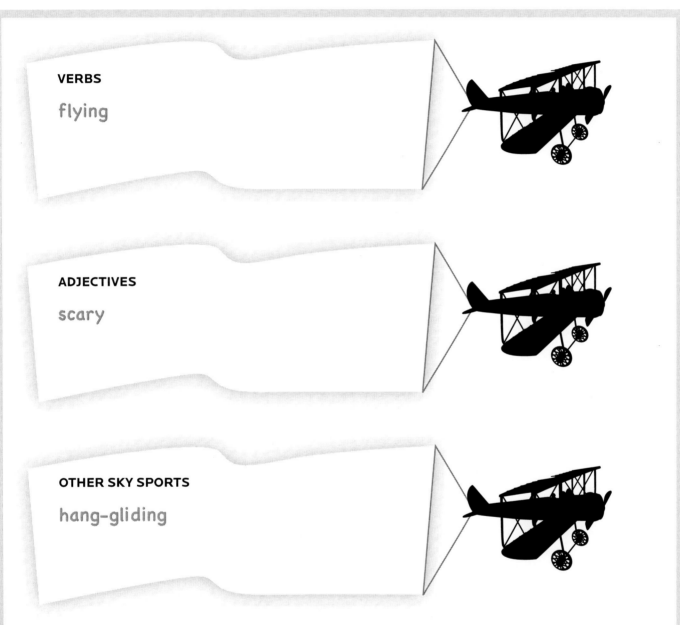

VERBS

flying

ADJECTIVES

scary

OTHER SKY SPORTS

hang-gliding

Add a fourth flag if you want to. Explain why you chose the words.

LARGEST SINOSAUROPTERYX FOSSIL

This persuasive text is in the form of a school poster advertising a science field trip to the Jurassic Coast. It includes the Guinness World Record for the largest Sinosauropteryx fossil.

Text type:	persuasion
AFs covered:	AF2, AF3, AF5, AF6
Specialist vocabulary:	Sinosauropteryx, creature, Jurassic, equipment, geological, belemnites, ammonites

ANSWERS

ON YOUR MARKS

a. Fossils are the remains of creatures from the distant past. *Literal AF2*

b. You might need waterproof clothes to keep you dry in bad weather. *Deduction AF3*

c. You might need a plastic bag to keep your notebook dry. *Inference AF3*

GET SET

a. The fossil hunters are going to the Jurassic Coast. *Literal AF2*

b. Special equipment is being provided because they are unlikely to already have it. *Inference AF3*

c. The author wants the reader to feel a sense of urgency about the need to sign up for the trip. *Inference AF6*

GO FOR GOLD!

a. The largest Sinosauropteryx fossil is kept at the Shandong Tianyu Natural History Museum in Shandong province, China. *Literal AF2*

b. Distant past means a very long time ago. *Deduction AF5*

c. The poster encourages readers to go on the trip by using powerful vocabulary, a question, an imperative verb and statements such as 'Fossils are fascinating' and 'history of life on Earth'. It makes you feel included by saying that anyone is welcome but also makes you feel you will be special if you go by saying that places are limited. *Inference AF6*

BEYOND THE RECORD

Use the internet or an atlas to find where the Jurassic Coast is. Find out why it was given this name.

Background research, reading and discussion to help the children to prepare

- Ask the children what they already know about the Jurassic Coast. Discuss what they think it looks like and what they would be able to see or find there.

- Guide children to websites such as www.nationaltrust.org.uk/jurassic-coast/, http://jurassiccoast.org/ and www.rgs.org/OurWork/Schools/Geography+in+the+News/Ask+the+experts/Jurassic+Coast.htm.

- If appropriate, provide hard-copy atlases and maps.

Recording their ideas

- How will the children record their findings about the location of the Jurassic Coast? Will they print out a detailed map, or mark up where the coast is on a map of the UK? How will they make notes about the Jurassic Coast and why it was given this name? In a word-processed document; on paper?

LANGUAGE ACTIVITY WORKSHEET

- This worksheet can be used to introduce the concept of proofreading and the use of a dictionary when children are unsure of a spelling.

- Explain that there are 10 spelling and punctuation mistakes in the text and that it needs to be thoroughly proofread.

- Encourage the children to read through the text, using dictionaries to double check any words they are unsure of, rather than looking at the Pupil Book.

Answers: wanted, creatures, add full stop after *past*, fascinating, history, Earth, pencil, welcome, geological, add closing bracket after *gloves*.

PROOFREADING FOR EXPLORERS!

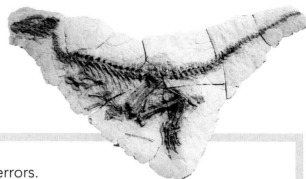

This school poster has 10 spelling and punctuation errors.
Proofread the text and correct the mistakes.

YOUNG FOSSIL HUNTERS WANTID!

Fossils are the remains of creetures that lived in the distant past Fossils are fasinating. They can tell us about the histry of life on erth.

A visit to the Jurassic Coast is planned for the next science field trip.

You will need:

- warm, waterproof clothes
- strong, non-slip boots or shoes
- a notebook and pensil
- a plastic bag in case the weather is wet.

Anyone interested in becoming a fossil hunter is wellcome.

Special equipment (geologicol hammers, picks, goggles and gloves will be provided by the school.

LARGEST MASK

This sightseeing information-style text is about the Guinness World Record for the largest mask, which was made as part of the 2011 Xanthi carnival in Greece.

Text type:	non-chronological report/recount
AFs covered:	AF2, AF3
Specialist vocabulary:	carnival, Greece, mask, Styrofoam, carved, character

ANSWERS

ON YOUR MARKS

a. Xanthi is in the north of Greece. *Literal AF2*

b. *Personal opinion AF3*

c. The artist chose to make a record-breaking mask so he could be a Guinness World Record holder. *Personal opinion AF3*

GET SET

a. The mask was made of blue and white Styrofoam. *Literal AF2*

b. It took so long because the artist had to cut 150 pieces of Styrofoam into different shapes and then stick them all together. *Inference AF3*

c. The mask was made from something light and flexible so it could be easily shaped and displayed. *Deduction AF3*

GO FOR GOLD!

a. First, the artist cut 150 pieces of Styrofoam, then he and a team stuck them together. Next, he carved out the back and made holes for the eyes and mouth. *Literal AF2*

b. The mask was unveiled in a sports centre because it was so large it needed lots of space. *Inference AF3*

c. The mask was of a story character because the character was well known to most people. *Deduction AF3*

BEYOND THE RECORD

Find three very different types of mask that have been worn by different people for different purposes. What mask would you like to wear and what would you do when wearing it?

Background research, reading and discussion to help the children to prepare

- Discuss and list the many different uses of a mask, e.g. protection, disguise, ceremonial, entertainment.
- As a class, search online for images of masks.
- Guide the children to websites such as: en.wikipedia.org/wiki/Mask; http://42explore.com/mask.htm; www.masksoftheworld.com.

Recording their ideas

- Encourage the children to decide how to record notes about their three masks. Will they use images with captions, a Mind Map™, a simple list, sticky notes?
- Ask them to choose the mask they would like to wear and write down the reasons for their choice – its use, shape, material, design, origin or another reason?
- Encourage them to discuss their choice in small groups or present their choice to the rest of the class.

LANGUAGE ACTIVITY WORKSHEET

- This worksheet can be used to introduce the use of inverted commas for direct speech. Encourage the children to read out the example at the top of the sheet. Explain that the inverted commas are used to show the reader that someone is saying something.
- Point out that the last set of inverted commas comes after the comma. Explain to the children that inverted commas also come after other punctuation marks such as full stops, question marks and exclamation marks.
- Encourage the children to underline the direct speech used in the adapted text from a Greek folk tale about Karagiozis and then insert the missing inverted commas. Fast finishers can then move onto the second task at the bottom of the sheet.
- Once they have completed the task, encourage the children to read out the text in small groups, with each child taking the part of a different character.

Answers: 'What shall we carry it in?'; 'Your buckets!'; 'It's too hot to carry them,'; 'Then jump in the water to cool off,'; 'We can't swim,'; 'Then watch the fishes and learn to swim!'

KARAGIOZIS AND THE HOT DAY

We use inverted commas (' ') to show when a person is speaking.
'I need a long, cool drink of water,' said Karagiozis.

Underline the direct speech (the spoken words) in the story below and put in the missing inverted commas.

The first one is done for you.

It was a very hot day and Karagiozis was feeling thirsty.

'<u>Bring me some water,</u>' he told his three sons.

What shall we carry it in? asked his eldest son.

Your buckets! answered Karagiozis crossly.

It's too hot to carry them, moaned the middle son.

Then jump in the water to cool off, snapped Karagiozis.

We can't swim, said the youngest son.

Rewrite this text as a sentence with inverted commas.
Then watch the fishes and learn to swim!

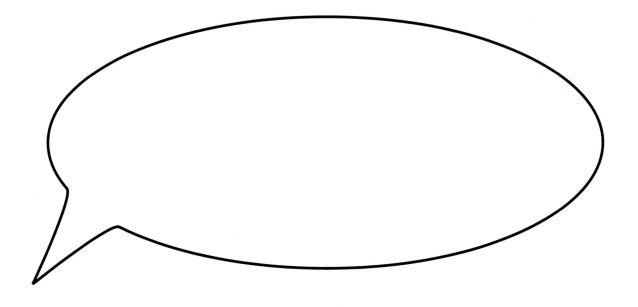

NARROWEST STREET

This non-chronological report about the narrowest streets in the world is in the style of a page from a travel magazine. It includes information about Spreuerhofstrasse, in Reutlingen, Germany.

Text type:	non-chronological report
AFs covered:	AF2, AF3, AF5
Specialist vocabulary:	narrowest, narrow, squeeze, widest, widened, street, Europe

ANSWERS

ON YOUR MARKS

a. The name of the world's narrowest street is Spreuerhofstrasse. *Literal AF2*

b. It is hard to walk down because the gap between the two walls is very narrow. *Inference AF3*

c. *Personal opinion AF3*

GET SET

a. The world's narrowest street is 31 cm at its narrowest point. *Literal AF2*

b. The gaps were made between the new houses to stop fire spreading quickly. *Inference AF3*

c. People use Parliament Street as a shortcut between Waterbeer Street and the High Street. *Deduction AF3*

GO FOR GOLD!

a. In 1726, a large fire in the city destroyed many of the houses. *Literal AF2*

b. A large lunch could make your tummy bigger, which would make it harder to walk down the narrow street. *Inference AF3, AF5*

c. *Personal opinion AF3*

BEYOND THE RECORD

Imagine you are a film director trying to find a narrow street to use in a spooky scene. What three questions would you ask about Spreuerhofstrasse? Who would you ask?

Background research, reading and discussion to help the children to prepare

- Search online for images of a spooky street (try typing 'spooky street' into a Google images search) and, if possible, a suitable clip of a spooky street scene from a film or TV show.

- Look at the various images or the film clip. Discuss with the children what makes a spooky scene on film. List the ideas. Apart from the atmosphere, what else would a film production company need?

- Discuss to whom the film director would pose the questions. In what ways could the questions be asked, e.g. email, letter, verbally?

Recording their ideas

- Encourage the children to decide how they are going to record ideas for their questions: a Mind Map™, sticky notes, lists?

- How will they make the final choice for the three questions? Will they debate it within a group/in pairs?

Ideas for questions may include: What access is there for film equipment? Can the site be closed off from the public? When is the best time to film? Is there space for props and lighting equipment? What times are allowed for filming?

LANGUAGE ACTIVITY WORKSHEET

- This worksheet allows revision and reinforcement of the rules that explain comparative suffixes -*er* and -*est*. Provide the children with the worksheet and remind them how they can add the suffixes -*er* and -*est* to adjectives and adverbs to compare people and things with each other.

- Work through the four rules and the examples shown on the worksheet. Discuss any questions the children may have. Allow them to complete the worksheet and discuss their answers with a partner or within a small group.

- Encourage the children to continue adding more of their own comparative words on a separate piece of paper. Discuss their choices. Have they followed the rules correctly? Do they need more support?

Answers: shorter, soft; loudest, quieter, quietest; funniest; wetter.

OFFICIALLY AMAZING

MAKING SENSE OF SUFFIXES

We add the suffixes -er and -est onto adjectives and adverbs when we want to compare things or people with each other.

Write the missing words in the gaps.

The suffix -er should be used when you are comparing just two things.

tall	taller
short	
	softer

The suffix -est should be used when you are comparing more than two things.

narrow	narrower	narrowest
loud	louder	
quiet		

For two-syllable words ending in y, drop the y and add i before -er and -est.

happy	happier	happiest
funny	funnier	

For one-syllable words, double the last letter before -er or -est.

big	bigger	biggest
wet		wettest

What other words follow these patterns?
Add your own words on a separate piece of paper.

MOST SPOONS BALANCED ON THE FACE

This information and instructions text is in the style of a TV script. It is about Aaron Caissie, who broke the Guinness World Record for the most spoons balanced on the face on 18 April 2009.

Text type:	recount/instructions
AFs covered:	AF2, AF3, AF4, AF6
Specialist vocabulary:	spoon, balancing, script, breathe, seventeen, rehearsal

ANSWERS

ON YOUR MARKS

a. Aaron put 17 spoons on his face. *Literal AF2*

b. *Personal opinion AF3*

c. If you leaned your face back, it would help keep the spoons on your face. *Inference AF3*

GET SET

a. Aaron broke the record on *Lo Show dei Record*. *Literal AF2*

b. Bullet points are used to list the rules clearly. *Deduction AF4*

c. Soup spoons are wider than other spoons so are easier to balance. *Inference AF3*

GO FOR GOLD!

a. Joe Allison from Britain held the record before Aaron. *Literal AF2*

b. *Personal opinion AF3*

c. Brackets are used to show instructions for the people working on the TV programme. *Deduction AF4*

BEYOND THE RECORD

Plan your own balancing challenge. Write a set of rules and tips. How will you present the information to your group or class?

Background research, reading and discussion to help the children to prepare

- Provide children with access to balancing information from online sources, such as www.wikihow.com/Category:Balancing-Tricks.

- Discuss why a proper challenge needs rules. Briefly talk about the types of balancing that could be used for a challenge, e.g. balancing objects on the body or something else, perhaps balancing on something themselves.

- Revise the organisational features used for instructions, e.g. numbered lists, imperative verbs, concise sentences. Talk about them or list the features so that the children can see and refer to them.

- How will they decide on the rules and tips? Will they take information from resources or try out the challenge first?

Recording their ideas

- Encourage the children to decide how to record their ideas for a balancing challenge: with handwritten notes, sticky notes, on the computer, using a Mind Map™, creating a poster with sketches?

- Encourage the children to choose their form of presentation. Ideas include a poster, rules and tips booklet, comic strip with captions for rules. How will they present their rules to the class? Using an overhead projector or visualiser? Or a computer application such as Microsoft PowerPoint®?

Feedback: Discuss which set of rules and tips were clear and easy to follow and why this was.

LANGUAGE ACTIVITY WORKSHEET

- This worksheet looks at how the suffix *-ly* turns adjectives to adverbs. Remind the children that an adjective describes a noun, e.g. a *sad* clown. Discuss what an adverb is. Show how most adjectives can be turned into adverbs when the suffix *-ly* is added, e.g. he *sadly* walked.

- Encourage the children to read out the two rules for adding *-ly* to adjectives to make them into adverbs.

- Once the children have completed the worksheet, reinforce the two *-ly* rules again and identify the children who may need extra support. For more able children, discuss the exceptions to the rule for *-ly*.

Answers: angrily, sadly, deeply, hungrily, strongly, cheerfully, heavily, helpfully.

ADJECTIVES TO ADVERBS

- Add -ly onto the end of an adjective to make it an adverb: *poor – poorly, hopeful – hopefully.*
- If the adjective ends with *y*, then change the *y* to *i* and then add -ly: *happy – happ i ly – happily.*

Turn the eight adjectives below into adverbs. Write each adverb on a spoon.

angry   sad   deep   hungry   strong   cheerful   heavy   helpful

Now write two of your own adverbs on these spoons.

Choose an adverb from one of the spoons to use in a sentence. Write your sentence here.

_____

_____

MOST CONSECUTIVE HAIRCUTS BY A TEAM IN EIGHT HOURS

This blog-style recount and information text is about a hairdressing team from the Cre8 salon in Cape Coral, Florida, USA, who broke the Guinness World Record for the most consecutive haircuts by a team in eight hours.

Text type:	recount
AFs covered:	AF2, AF3, AF6
Specialist vocabulary:	consecutive, hairdresser, salon, hair, scissors, queue, sore

ANSWERS

ON YOUR MARKS

a. Family, friends and local people came to have their hair cut. *Literal AF2*
b. The salon needed getting ready because the hairdressers had to cut hair for many hours. *Inference AF3*
c. The writer seemed excited and happy to be part of the day. *Deduction AF6*

GET SET

a. The Cre8 Salon is in Cape Coral, Florida, USA. *Literal AF2*
b. The day was like a party because so many people came along and there was food and music. *Inference AF3*
c. Some haircuts were not allowed because they weren't finished or proper haircuts. *Deduction AF3*

GO FOR GOLD!

a. 'Consecutive' means one after another. *Literal AF2*
b. The writer is writing about the event to share it with other people, who may not have been able to take part. *Deduction AF6*
c. *Personal opinion AF2, AF3*

BEYOND THE RECORD

After they broke the record, the Cre8 team were interviewed on TV. Imagine you are the interviewer. Write down five questions you would like to ask the hairdressers.

Background research, reading and discussion to help the children to prepare

- Discuss why TV interviewers would ask the stylists questions, e.g. to give on-the-spot information for the viewer, to ask questions that viewers would like to have asked if they were at the event.
- Guide children to specific websites to find out more about the Cre8 record attempt, such as http://cre8salon.com/media/.
- Find and show suitable clips of TV interviews for the children to watch (examples can be found on the *Newsround* website: www.bbc.co.uk/newsround/).

Recording their ideas

- Encourage the children to write down as many questions as they like. How will they choose the final five questions?

Ideas for questions may include: Who came up with the idea for the record? What was it like having to follow such strict rules when cutting the hair? What was the atmosphere like? How did you keep going? When did you know you had broken the record? What will you do next?

LANGUAGE ACTIVITY WORKSHEET

- This worksheet revises three different sentence forms: statement, question and exclamation. Encourage the children to read the three definitions at the top of the worksheet. Ask them to give oral examples of the different sentence forms.
- After the children have completed the first task of adding the correct punctuation, encourage them to think of one question they would like to ask about hair and then to write down one statement about their own hair (this could be about style, colour or texture).

Answers: question, exclamation, full stop, question, exclamation, full stop, question, full stop, exclamation.

OFFICIALLY AMAZING

HAIR-RAISING SENTENCES

Statement sentences end with a full stop (.).
Question sentences end with a question mark (?).
Exclamation sentences end with an exclamation mark (!).

The sentences below are missing a full stop, question mark or exclamation mark. Add in the right punctuation and then write down what type of sentence it is. The first one has been done for you.

1. A head of hair can hold the weight of two whole African elephants!   *exclamation*

2. How many hairs are there on a normal head of hair   _____

3. Oh no, I can lose up to 90 hairs a day   _____

4. Some Ancient Greek women had dyed red hair,
   sprinkled with gold powder   _____

5. Where does the word 'shampoo' come from   _____

6. Rapunzel, your hair is so incredibly long   _____

7. The Guinness World Record for the longest female hair is 5.627 m   _____

8. How long does hair grow in a day   _____

9. Hair grows faster in warm weather   _____

10. Our teacher dyed her hair pink   _____

Write down one question you would like to ask about hair.

_____

_____

Write down one statement about your own hair.

_____

_____

© Rising Stars UK Ltd. 2013   Record-Breaking Comprehension/Year 3/Most consecutive haircuts by a team in eight hours

HEAVIEST CAR BALANCED ON THE HEAD

This formal letter is written by a school boy to John Evans, the Guinness World Record holder of the heaviest car balanced on the head.

Text type:	formal letter
AFs covered:	AF2, AF3, AF4, AF5
Specialist vocabulary:	heaviest, balance, second, sincerely, gutted

ANSWERS

ON YOUR MARKS

a. **John balanced a Mini car on his head.** *Literal AF2*

b. **Imran finds it hard to balance a ball on his head because it easily rolls off.** *Inference AF3*

c. **This is a letter because of the address and the date at the top, and the use of 'Dear' at the start and 'Yours sincerely' at the end.** *Deduction AF4*

GET SET

a. **Imran's favourite record is heaviest car balanced on the head.** *Literal AF2*

b. **Imran wrote the letter because he is doing a topic on balancing at school and wants to find out more.** *Inference AF3*

c. **John doesn't like to balance a car when it is windy as the wind can push against the car, making it much harder to balance and much more dangerous.** *Deduction AF3*

GO FOR GOLD!

a. **Any two from: crates, bricks, bikes, beds, boats, fridges and cars.** *Literal AF2*

b. **This is a formal letter because Imran has used formal words and the layout you would expect of a formal letter.** *Deduction AF4, AF5*

c. *Personal opinion AF3*

BEYOND THE RECORD

Use the internet to find out more about John Evans. Choose one of his other records and write a newspaper report about his attempt. Remember to include the what, when, where, who, why and how.

Background research, reading and discussion to help the children to prepare

• Using examples, discuss the features of writing a newspaper report with the children (the five Ws).

• Direct children to John Evans' website at www.headbalancer.com (it is worth familiarising yourself with this content beforehand). You may also wish to point children to online newspaper reports or video clips.

Recording their ideas

• How are the children going to work? Individually, as partners or in groups? If in groups, will they give each other different aspects of the news article to focus on or work as one?

• Encourage the children to decide how they will record information about their chosen record: note taking, printing off information and highlighting, using a Mind Map™, etc.

• How is the newspaper report going to be created? By computer or by hand? Will it have pictures?

LANGUAGE ACTIVITY WORKSHEET

• This worksheet helps reinforce the learning of *eigh*, *ey* and *ei* words with the *ai* sound. Write out the word *neighbour* for the children to see. Underline the *eigh* in the word and ask the children to say its sound (*ai*). As a class, sound out the whole word. Repeat for an *ey* and *ei* word.

• Tell the children that they are going to look at words with the letters *eigh*, *ey* and *ei* that sound like *ai*. The wordsearch will help children to recognise the spellings, while organising the words into *eigh*, *ey* and *ei* groups will help them to notice the patterns.

• Once they have completed the worksheet, encourage the children to discuss what other *eigh*, *ey* and *ei* words they have found that also have the *ai* sound. Discuss possible strategies that will help them remember these words, e.g. look, cover, write, check; rhymes, etc.

Answers: eight, weigh, sleigh, neigh; rein; they, grey.

**OFFICIALLY
AMAZING**

BALANCING EIGH, EY AND EI WORDS

Some words include the letters *eigh*, *ei* and *ey*, which all sound like *ai*.

Find the seven words in the wordsearch and then write them in the correct car.

w	e	i	g	h	s
t	n	l	r	p	l
g	r	e	y	c	e
p	i	s	i	m	i
n	r	a	b	g	g
e	i	g	h	t	h
t	h	e	y	s	j

rein
weigh
they
neigh
sleigh
eight
grey

Add one more *eigh*, *ey* and *ei* word to each car.

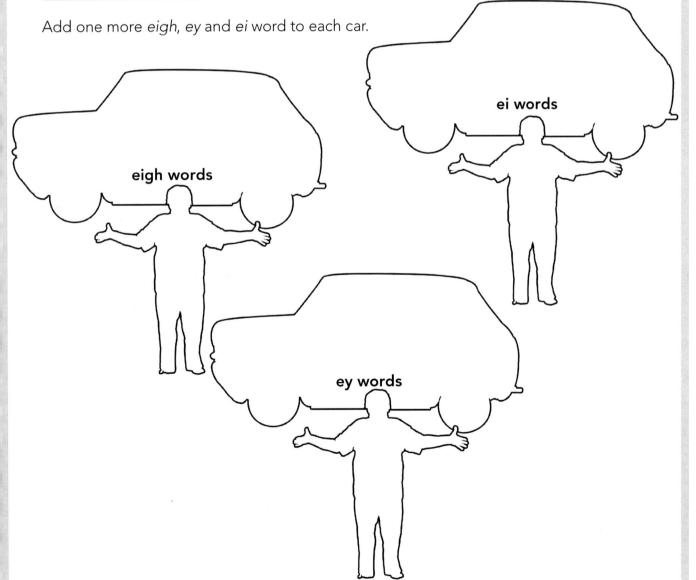

eigh words

ei words

ey words

LARGEST ORCHESTRA PLAYING ON RECYCLED MATERIALS

This persuasive poster-style text encourages festival-goers to try and break the Guinness World Record for the largest orchestra playing on recycled materials.

Text type:	persuasion
AFs covered:	AF2, AF3, AF4, AF5, AF6
Specialist vocabulary:	orchestra, festival, recycled, material, musical, instrument

ANSWERS

ON YOUR MARKS

a. **The world record is the largest orchestra playing on recycled materials.** *Literal AF2*

b. **Oil drums would make good instruments because they make a loud, musical sound.** *Inference AF3*

c. *Personal opinion AF3*

GET SET

a. **Woodbridge Festival is one of the biggest summer music festivals in Europe.** *Literal AF2*

b. **The poster is colourful with clear headings and a list saying how you can help. The poster also includes a question and persuasive language to make you want to join in with the record attempt and support recycling.** *Inference AF4, AF5, AF6*

c. *Personal opinion AF3*

GO FOR GOLD!

a. **1,235 people hold the current record for the largest orchestra playing on recycled materials.** *Literal AF2*

b. **The workshops would help the players by giving them a chance to learn their piece and work out how best to play their recycled instruments.** *Deduction AF3*

c. **The aims of the poster are to gather enough people to break the Guinness World Record and to show everyone how important recycling is.** *Inference AF3*

BEYOND THE RECORD

Draw a design for your own recycled instrument. Use labels to show what it is made of, how it works and what sound it makes.

Background research, reading and discussion to help the children to prepare

- As a class, search online for images of recycled instruments to gather ideas. (You could carry out a Google Images search with the search term 'recycled instruments'.)

- Using the images as a reference, discuss the different types of materials that could be used to create different instruments. How do they help make a sound (e.g. large empty tin for a resonating drum)?

Recording their ideas

- Encourage the children to think about how they will record their initial ideas, e.g. rough sketches and notes or labels.

- Emphasise the need for the information to be clear and easy to read.

Ideas for labels may include: use of materials to make different sounds; technical vocabulary, e.g. vibration; type of instrument – wind, string, percussion, brass; vocabulary to explain sounds.

LANGUAGE ACTIVITY WORKSHEET

- This worksheet looks at the use of the *to have* verb to mark the relationships of time and cause. Read the example at the top of the sheet. Ask the children if this sentence is in the past or present tense.

- Discuss how the *to have* verb can show when the action took place. Highlight the second part of the sentence and discuss how it shows why the action took place.

- Once the children have completed the worksheet, encourage them to check their work with others. Discuss how it is important to get the right tense for the *to have* verb for the sentences to make sense.

Answers: Alfie <u>has</u> turned off the tap <u>so that he can save water</u>. Sky <u>had</u> made a scarf out of wool by teatime <u>so he would be warm</u>. I <u>have</u> built a compost bin <u>as a way to help my garden grow</u>. Anil will <u>have</u> sold all his old toys by the end of the day <u>to make extra money</u>! I <u>have</u> put newspaper on the table <u>so we can paint our model</u>.

OFFICIALLY AMAZING

REDUCE, RE-USE, RECYCLE

We can put *had*, *have* or *has* in front of action verbs to show when the action is done and why it happens.

Abdul _had_ thrown his plastic bottle in the green bin <u>so it could be recycled.</u>

Read the sentences and write in either *had*, *have* or *has*.

Underline the part of the sentence that shows why the action took place.

The first one has been done for you.

Ying **has** bought a bin <u>for us to put paper in</u>.

Alfie _____ turned off the tap so that he can save water.

Sky _____ made a scarf out of old wool by teatime so he would be warm.

I _____ built a compost bin as a way to help my garden grow.

Anil will _____ sold all his old toys by the end of the day to make extra money!

I _____ put newspaper on the table so we can paint our model.

Write a sentence about recycling using either *have*, *has* or *had*.

_____

_____

_____

_____

MOST PEOPLE READING ALOUD SIMULTANEOUSLY – SINGLE LOCATION

This email-style recount text is written from the perspective of a child who helped to break the Guinness World Record for most people reading aloud simultaneously, in Turkey.

Text type:	recount
AFs covered:	AF2, AF3, AF5, AF6
Specialist vocabulary:	simultaneously, stadium, volunteer, ticket, chapter, aloud

ANSWERS

ON YOUR MARKS

a. **23,822 people broke the world record.** *Literal AF2*

b. **You can tell this is an email from the** *To:,* **cc: and** *Subject:* **fields.** *Deduction AF4*

c. *Personal opinion AF2, AF3*

GET SET

a. **The book Habib read from was called** *Les Misérables.* *Literal AF2*

b. **It sounded 'awesome' because thousands of people were reading the book aloud at the same time.** *Inference AF3, AF5*

c. **It was 'incredible news' because the event involved so many people and because Habib had become a Guinness World Record holder.** *Deduction AF6*

GO FOR GOLD!

a. **Habib was given a ticket when he arrived at the stadium.** *Literal AF2*

b. **Habib found it spooky because a stadium full of people would normally be very loud but it was completely silent.** *Inference AF3, AF5*

c. *Personal opinion AF2, AF3*

BEYOND THE RECORD

Research the Malatya Inönü Stadium on the internet. Produce a fact sheet about it. Find out about three other stadiums around the world and add the information to your fact sheet.

Background research, reading and discussion to help the children to prepare

- Explain that the word *stadium* means a venue for large events such as sports events and concerts. Discuss who would want to read a fact sheet on stadiums. What information would they expect?

- As a class, search Wikipedia (en.wikipedia.org/) for Malatya Inönü Stadium.

- Guide children to websites with information on world stadiums: www.worldstadiums.com/; en.wikipedia.org/wiki/List_of_stadiums_by_capacity; www.topendsports.com/events/summer/stadiums.htm.

Recording their ideas

- What style of fact sheet are they going to produce: paragraphs with sub-headings, headings with simple bulleted facts? Will they use any images?

- Encourage the children to think about how they will record the information they find out from websites, e.g. using sticky notes, drawing a rough layout of the fact sheet and writing in notes.

Ideas may include: location, capacity, the number of seats, when it was built, types of events, famous events, design.

LANGUAGE ACTIVITY WORKSHEET

- This worksheet allows the children to practise proofreading a text for commonly misspelled words. Provide the children with the worksheet and explain that 10 of the words have been misspelled. It is their task to proofread the text to locate and underline the 10 mistakes.

- They must then write out the correct spellings in the spelling box under the text. Allow access to dictionaries and word banks to help them. When the children have found and corrected the mistakes, they could self-mark or mark another's work, using the text from the Pupil Book.

Answers: knews (news), peple (people), famly (family), uther (other), arrivd (arrived), realy (really), hole (whole), red (read), droped (dropped), wold (world).

**OFFICIALLY
AMAZING**

HABIB'S SPELL CHECK

Habib has made 10 spelling mistakes in his email. Proofread the text and underline the wrong spellings. Write the correct spellings in the box under the text. Don't look at the original text until you have checked your work.

⚫ ⚪ ⚪   **New Message**

Send   Chat   Attach   Address   Fonts   Colors   Save As Draft   Photo Browser   Show Stationery

To: Thea

Cc:

Subject: I am a Guinness World Record holder!

                                                        Signature: None

Hi Thea,

Have incredible knews! Remember this date – **12 May 2011** – because that's when I became a Guinness World Record holder. It's true.

Volunteers were needed to try to set a new Guinness World Record for the most peple reading aloud simultaneously in one place. By the way, 'simultaneously' means at the same time.

So, on 12 May, my famly and I caught a bus to the Malatya Inönü Stadium, Turkey, along with hundreds of uther people.

When we arrivd at the stadium, we were given a ticket and checked to see if we had the right book. Next, we were shown into the arena, where thousands of people were waiting. It was realy noisy but very exciting.

Just then, someone asked for quiet and the hole stadium went silent. It was spooky.

After that, we all red the first chapter from *Les Misérables* by Victor Hugo, in Turkish. It sounded awesome.

Finally, as we walked out, we droped our tickets into a box so they could be counted to see how many people had read.

So, the new wold record is … **23,822! Hurray!**

Best wishes,

Habib

Correct spellings

1. _____   2. _____   3. _____   4. _____

5. _____   6. _____   7. _____   8. _____

9. _____   10. _____

TALLEST SUNFLOWER

This explanation text gives advice on how to grow and care for sunflowers as well as information about the Guinness World Record for the tallest sunflower.

Text type:	explanation/non-chronological report
AFs covered:	**AF2, AF3, AF4, AF6**
Specialist vocabulary:	**tallest, sunflower, plant, field, giant, pith**

ANSWERS

ON YOUR MARKS

a. Hans-Peter Schiffer grew the world's tallest sunflower. *Literal AF2*

b. Sunflowers need special plant food to help them grow tall and strong. *Inference AF3*

c. Sunflowers 'follow' the sun so they can get lots of sunlight. *Deduction AF3*

GET SET

a. The world's tallest sunflower was 8.03 m. *Literal AF2*

b. The stems of heavy sunflowers could bend or break due to the weight of the flowers. *Inference AF3*

c. The layout has clear sub-headings to tell the reader where to find information. *Deduction AF4*

GO FOR GOLD!

a. The world's tallest sunflower was grown in Kaarst-Voorst, Germany, on 17 August 2009. *Literal AF2*

b. Sunflower pith was used in life jackets because it was so light and would help the wearer to float. *Inference AF3*

c. *Personal opinion AF6*

BEYOND THE RECORD

Use the information in the text to draw diagrams and captions to show how giant sunflowers are grown. Present your diagrams to the class and then hold a question-and-answer session.

Background research, reading and discussion to help the children to prepare

• If possible, show some examples of diagrams and captions of plants from printed gardening books or online sources. Discuss the effectiveness and features of each style, e.g. short sentence captions, labels.

• With the children, discuss different methods of finding the information that they need in a text, e.g. skimming and scanning.

Recording their ideas

• Encourage the children to decide how they are going to retrieve the information they will need from the text. Will they make notes, underline the text, use sticky notes, etc?

• How will they present their diagrams: in a hand-drawn poster, by scanning their artwork and adding labels using a computer? Remind them that their labels should be clear for others to follow and read.

Ideas may include: the best place to grow seeds and why, the care needed for growing sunflowers, the different parts of a sunflower.

LANGUAGE ACTIVITY WORKSHEET

• Use the worksheet to encourage children to think about how they could make their vocabulary more varied and rich within their writing. Provide printed or online thesauruses. Choose a word such as *hot* and demonstrate how the thesaurus can give other words that have the same meaning.

• Point to the worksheet and explain that the children need to find adjectives that have the same meanings. Encourage them to use a thesaurus to help them.

• Once they have completed the worksheet, talk about their favourite adjectives for each sunflower. Discuss how some words can create better images or messages for the reader.

Answers: Possible words include (huge) large, enormous, massive, giant; (small) tiny, little, wee, teeny; (sunny) summery, fine, clear, warm; (windy) blowy, blustery, gusty, stormy.

GROWING ADJECTIVES

In the middle of each flower there is an adjective (a describing word).
In the petals, write other adjectives that have the same meaning.
Use a thesaurus to help you.

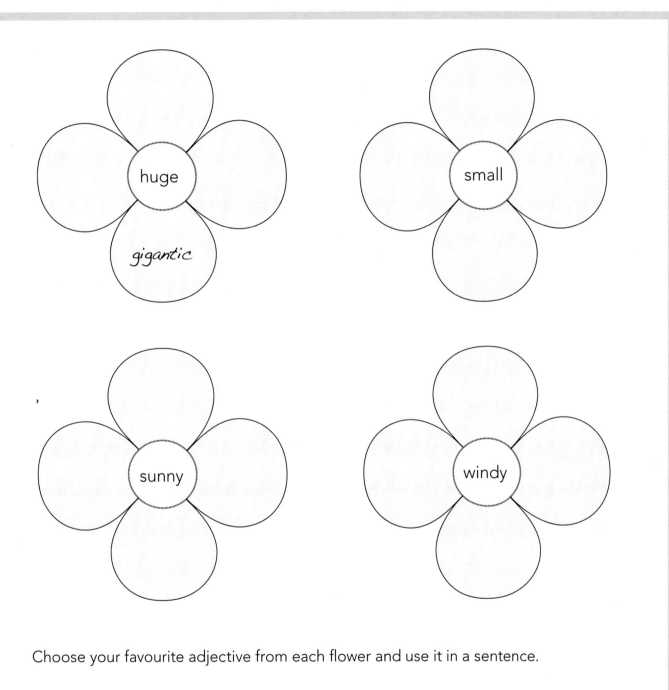

huge

gigantic

small

sunny

windy

Choose your favourite adjective from each flower and use it in a sentence.

_____

_____

_____

_____

LONGEST TONGUE

This magazine-style text, aimed at children, provides fun facts about the human tongue, including information about the Guinness World Record for the longest tongue, held by Stephen Taylor.

Text type:	explanation
AFs covered:	**AF2, AF3**
Specialist vocabulary:	**tongue, saliva, taste, swallow, muscle, bitter**

ANSWERS

ON YOUR MARKS

a. The tongue helps you chew, taste, swallow and talk. *Literal AF2*
b. You need a mirror to look at your tongue because you can't look down and see it. *Inference AF3*
c. The blue whale has a huge tongue because it is a very large creature. *Deduction AF3*

GET SET

a. Every person has a different tongue print. *Literal AF2*
b. Stephen has stuck his tongue out so much to show people how long it is. *Inference AF3*
c. *Personal opinion AF3*

GO FOR GOLD!

a. You would measure the length of your tongue from its tip to the middle of your closed top lip. *Literal AF2*
b. A tongue needs to be strong to help us chew, swallow, talk and taste. *Inference AF3*
c. It is a tongue twister because it has lots of similar sounds, and when you say it out loud, the words can get twisted. *Deduction AF3*

BEYOND THE RECORD

Use books and the internet to find out about two or three animals, insects or mammals who have long or large tongues. Find out why they have long tongues and how they use them. How will you record the information you find out: as diagrams with labels, or using bullet points?

Background research, reading and discussion to help the children to prepare

- Collect reference books/wildlife magazines, etc. for children to refer to.
- Guide children to websites such as www.environmentalgraffiti. com/ecology/amazing-versatility-animal-tongues/15016 and news.softpedia.com/news/Top-10-Weird-Tongues-83236.shtml. You may also wish to bookmark other relevant websites for use in class.

Recording their ideas

- Encourage the children to decide how to record their initial ideas: as a simple list, using sticky notes, as a Mind Map™, as written notes under simple headings?
- How will they record their completed work: as diagrams with labels, or using bullet points?
- How will they present their work: as a Microsoft PowerPoint® presentation, a poster, a written information and visual text that can be printed out or shown on a screen?

Ideas may include: what habitat the animals or insects live in, whether they are endangered, whether they need their tongues for other activities apart from eating, which creatures are the most fascinating.

LANGUAGE ACTIVITY WORKSHEET

- Use the worksheet to revisit or introduce alliteration. With the children, read out the tongue twister at the top of the worksheet. Explore more alliterative examples with the children, e.g. *Two tired tigers, Jolly jumping jellies.*
- Ask the children to choose words to create two tongue twisters.
- The children can then create their own tongue twister (check that it is alliterative). Discuss how alliteration can help them in their descriptive writing and poetry. Point out the use of adjectives, adverbs and verbs in alliterative sentences.

Answers: Gina Giraffe gracefully grazed on green grass; Sally Snake silently slithered along slippery stones.

TRICKY TONGUE TWISTERS

Look closely at this tongue twister.

She sells seashells on the seashore.

Most of the words start with the same letter, *s*. This is called alliteration.

Use the words below to make two tongue twisters.
Write them next to the correct animal.

~~Chas~~	grass	~~changed~~	stones
Gina	slippery	~~Chameleon~~	gracefully
on	silently	grazed	~~calmly~~
Giraffe	slithered	Snake	~~camouflage~~
green	Sally	along	~~colour~~

Chas Chameleon calmly
changed camouflage colour.

Write one of your own tongue twisters.

_____

_____

LARGEST HUMAN WHEELBARROW RACE

This TV news script recounts a successful bid to break the Guinness World Record for the largest human wheelbarrow race, by schools in Armidale in New South Wales, Australia.

Text type:	recount
AFs covered:	AF2, AF3, AF4
Specialist vocabulary:	wheelbarrow, human, practising, local, course, crowd, metre

ANSWERS

ON YOUR MARKS

a. **777 human wheelbarrows broke the world record.** *Literal AF2*

b. **The children practised for weeks.** *Literal AF2, personal opinion AF2*

c. **Some went slowly during the race because (list of possible answers): the wheelbarrow person was heavy to hold; they could not walk or run very fast; they were unsure where they were going; they had not practised enough.** *Deduction AF3*

GET SET

a. **The Armidale human wheelbarrow race was held in Australia.** *Literal AF2*

b. **The explanation is at the beginning so that people who don't know what a human wheelbarrow is can understand what the reporter is talking about.** *Inference AF3, AF4*

c. *Personal opinion AF3*

GO FOR GOLD!

a. **Some human wheelbarrows went quickly and some went slowly.** *Literal AF2*

b. **The event allowed the schools to get to know each other and work together.** *Inference AF3*

c. **You can tell that the text is a TV news script because the first line says it is the news and the report is set out like a script.** *Deduction AF4*

BEYOND THE RECORD

If your school was planning an event like this, what would you need to think about to make sure it was well organised? Create a Mind Map™ to note your ideas.

Background research, reading and discussion to help the children to prepare

• Collect printed materials from school or local community events and use these to stimulate discussion.

• Guide children to websites such as http://involver.org. uk/2009/09/school-council-event-planning-sheet/; www.tbalert. org/help/org/documents/SchoolsFundraisingAdvice.pdf; www.thebiglunch.com/.

• See the Guinness World Records website for further information about record applications: www.guinnessworldrecords.com/faq/.

Recording their ideas

• Encourage the children to work as a team. Will they elect a team leader? Do they have a clear purpose for their event?

• Encourage the children to choose someone to write their ideas on the Mind Map™. Where will the event be held? Who will be involved? When will it take place? What is needed?

• Allow each group to present their ideas. Decide as a class whether each event would be successful.

Ideas may include: publicity (posters, adverts, newsletters, invitations, local press), budgets and costs, entertainment, equipment needed, food and drink, volunteers to run the event.

LANGUAGE ACTIVITY WORKSHEET

• Use this worksheet to reinforce the strategy of looking for shorter words within longer words to help with tricky spellings. Write a long word, such as *together*, and ask the children to find shorter words within it. Underline the shorter words using different-coloured pens. Highlight the short word sounds and the overall word sound. Explain how this strategy can be used to work out difficult spellings.

• Once the children have completed the worksheet, encourage them to use a dictionary to see if their shorter words are correct. Ask the children to look at long words they find hard to spell and locate any shorter words within them.

Answers: Possible words include wheel, eel, bar, row, barrow, arrow; cup, up, board, boar, oar, boa; imp, port, or, an, ant, import.

WORDS WITHIN WORDS

Finding shorter words within long words can help with difficult spellings, e.g. *another – an, not, her, other.*

Find five short words hidden in each long word below to help the human wheelbarrows get to the finishing line.

wheelbarrow

_____ _____ _____ _____ _____

cupboard

_____ _____ _____ _____ _____

important

_____ _____ _____ _____ _____

Choose two long words that you find hard to spell and try to find short words within them. Challenge a partner to find short words too. Use a dictionary to help you.

_____

_____ _____ _____ _____

_____

_____ _____ _____ _____

MOST PEOPLE SKIPPING – SINGLE VENUE

The first newsletter extract is written to persuade school children to take part in a Guinness World Record attempt. The second newsletter extract is written to congratulate those who successfully broke the record.

Text type:	persuasion/recount
AFs covered:	AF2, AF3, AF4, AF6
Specialist vocabulary:	skipping, challenge, event, lesson, skill, congratulations

ANSWERS

ON YOUR MARKS

a. The children are being asked if they like skipping with a rope. *Literal AF2*

b. 'Let's get skipping' is in larger letters to try and get the children keen to start skipping. *Inference AF4*

c. The 'East Zone District' is an area in Singapore. *Deduction AF3*

GET SET

a. The school is getting ready by running skipping lessons every day during and after school. *Literal AF2*

b. 54 schools have been asked to take part as they are all schools in the East Zone District. *Inference AF3*

c. The author says that 'you might even become a world record holder' to encourage more people to take part. *Deduction AF6*

GO FOR GOLD!

a. The children should take part because they could get fit, learn a new skill and become a world record holder. *Literal AF2*

b. The school newsletter is a good way to tell children about the event because everyone in the school will receive a copy. *Inference AF3*

c. *Personal opinion AF3*

BEYOND THE RECORD

Think of a fun club that could teach others in your class new skills such as skipping, hula-hoop twisting, street dancing or magic tricks. Create a poster to advertise the club. Include information about when and where the club takes place and why people should join.

Background research, reading and discussion to help the children to prepare

• As a class, discuss the kind of clubs the children attend (both in school and out of school). Why do they go to these clubs? How often do they go? Emphasise that there are many different types of club that people can join.

• Talk about what makes an effective poster, e.g. persuasive vocabulary, proper nouns, strong headings, clear and concise words.

Recording their ideas

• How will the children work? If in pairs or small groups, how will they record their ideas for a club, e.g. a Mind Map™? Will they split up and then report back with their club idea? How will they decide on the final club idea? By discussion? By voting?

• Encourage children to take on different roles within their groups to manage specific elements of the poster, e.g. the layout, visual design, wording.

• Once the posters are finished, put them on display. Are the posters clear, informative and persuasive?

LANGUAGE ACTIVITY WORKSHEET

• This worksheet can be used to revise or develop skills in using time adverbs. Read out the statement at the top of the sheet and the example given. Explain that as well as describing verbs, some adverbs tell us when something happens. Encourage children to make up a few sentences using the time adverbs in the box before they underline those used in the posters.

• Before the children create their own poster, check that they understand the use of time adverbs.

Answers: next, now; soon, still, then.

WHAT'S THE TIME?

The time adverbs in the box tell us when something is happening, e.g.
I will be coming home <u>soon</u>.

When?
then   next   soon   still   now

Read the posters below for two school clubs.
Underline in red the time adverbs that tell us when the events happen.

• NEW • NEW • NEW • NEW • NEW •

STREET DANCING CLUB

TO BE HELD NEXT WEDNESDAY.

MEET IN THE HALL AT 3.30 PM

JOIN OUR CREW NOW!

• NEW • NEW • NEW • NEW • NEW •

CRAFT CLUB BACK SOON – FROM 1 MAY

Will still be held on Mondays

If you love sticking, making, knitting and painting then come to Oak Class at 12.15 pm.

Create your own school club poster using time adverbs to tell people when it is happening.

MOST FORWARD ROLLS IN ONE HOUR – INDIVIDUAL

This blog-style text gives the reader information about Ashrita Furman, who has broken and set more Guinness World Records than anyone else, including most forward rolls in one hour – individual.

Text type:	biography
AFs covered:	AF2, AF3, AF4, AF5
Specialist vocabulary:	hero, sculpture, favourite, article, individual, forward

ANSWERS

ON YOUR MARKS

a. Ashrita Furman comes from the USA. *Literal AF2*

b. Harry wants to write about Ashrita because he wants to tell others about him and his many records. *Inference AF3*

c. *Personal opinion AF3*

GET SET

a. Harry's favourite record is the most forward rolls in one hour. *Literal AF2*

b. Harry writes 'Yuck!' either because he doesn't like mashed potato or he doesn't like the sound of eating so much of it in one minute. *Deduction AF5*

c. *Personal opinion AF3*

GO FOR GOLD!

a. Harry found out about Ashrita Furman from a newspaper article in the *Daily Telegraph*. *Literal AF2*

b. Harry writes in an informal way because he is writing a blog for his friends and family to read. *Inference AF4*

c. *Personal opinion AF3*

BEYOND THE RECORD

- Use Ashrita's website to find out more about the different Guinness World Records he holds.
- Choose your favourite record, then imagine you are going to try to break the record. Write a step-by step training programme.

Background research, reading and discussion to help the children to prepare

- Visit Ashrita's website, www.ashrita.com, to familiarise yourself with its layout and information. You may want to decide in advance what area you would like the children to focus on, e.g. 'Currently held records', 'Full list of all Ashrita's records'.
- After the children have had time to explore Ashrita's records, read out and discuss the training suggestions in 'How to break a record'. What does a training programme need to show?

Recording their ideas

- Once the children have chosen their favourite record, allow them to create their own simple planning notes on ways to train for the attempt using lists, sticky notes, etc.
- Encourage the children to decide how they will present the training programme, e.g. as a poster, a booklet or leaflet, or Microsoft PowerPoint® presentation. What text features will they use to ensure the information is accessible and clear: headings, bullet points, numbered lists?

LANGUAGE ACTIVITY WORKSHEET

- This worksheet can be used to revise and build on previous work around prefixes. Remind the children how prefixes such as *un* can change the meaning of verbs or adjectives such as *unhappy* or *undress*. Point out how some prefixes can also change nouns to mean something slightly different, such as the prefix *bi*. With the children, list *bi* words such as *bicycle, biplane, biceps, binocular*. Discuss the meaning of *bi* (two).
- Ask the children to look at the worksheet, which focuses on the prefixes *super* and *tele*. Discuss the meaning of each prefix. Let the children write in the correct prefix to make new nouns. Encourage them to add in a *super* and *tele* word of their own in the two blank pancakes. Children could use a dictionary to help them.

Answers: telephone, superpower, superhero, supermarket, television, telescope. Possible words include superman, superglue, superstar, supernatural, telephoto, teleport, telepathy.

PREFIX PANCAKES

The prefix *super* means 'better than normal'.   **super** + star = **super**star

The prefix *tele* means 'from afar'.   **tele** + vision = **tele**vision

Write the prefix *super* or *tele* in the pancakes to make new words.

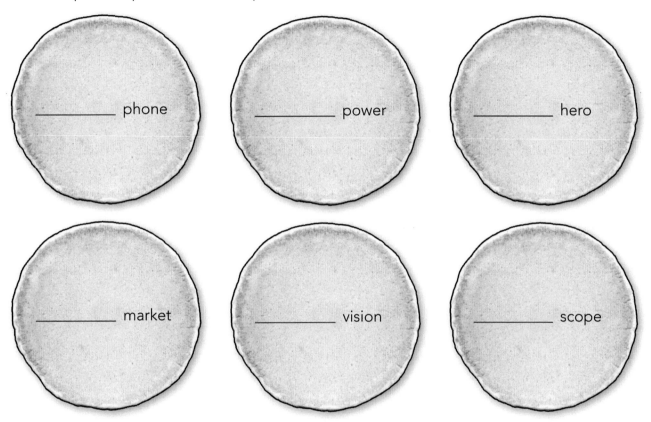

_____ phone   _____ power   _____ hero

_____ market   _____ vision   _____ scope

Add your own words using *super* and *tele* in the pancakes below.

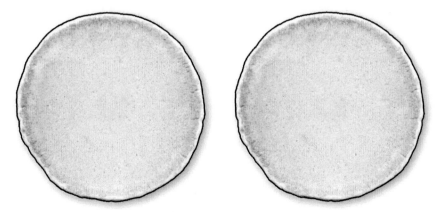

Choose one of the words and use it in a sentence.

_____

_____

FASTEST MARATHON CARRYING A 60-LB PACK

This website-style text is about Carl Andrew Creasey, who broke the Guinness World Record for the fastest marathon carrying a 60-lb pack.

Text type:	biography
AFs covered:	AF2, AF3, AF5
Specialist vocabulary:	marathon, distance, weights, training, commando, runner

ANSWERS

ON YOUR MARKS

a. Carl Andrew Creasey broke the record for the fastest marathon carrying a 60-lb pack. *Literal AF2*

b. Carl had to train so that he could get fit enough to carry his heavy pack in the marathon. *Deduction AF3*

c. Carl would have been very tired but really pleased that he had broken the world record. *Inference AF3*

GET SET

a. It took Carl 4 hours, 50 minutes, 56 seconds to finish the marathon. *Literal AF2*

b. The heat was the hardest part of the marathon because it would have made Carl hot and tired while he was running. *Inference AF3*

c. *Personal opinion AF3*

GO FOR GOLD!

a. Seeing a man with a certificate was 'a perfect end to the race' because it meant that after all his hard work, Carl had broken the record. *Literal AF2*

b. Carl meant that you can do anything that you put your mind to if you have a positive attitude. *Deduction AF5*

c. *Personal opinion AF3*

BEYOND THE RECORD

The type of measurements used here are 'imperial' measurements. We now use 'metric' measurements. Can you complete this chart?

Imperial	Metric
60 lb	
26 miles, 385 yards	

Background research, reading and discussion to help the children to prepare

- Write a list of imperial measurements, e.g. length (feet, inches), weight (ounces, pounds) and capacity (pints, gallons). Explain that these measurements were used by people in the past.

- Discuss practical ways of finding out the metric conversions.

- Guide the children to conversion websites such as www.onlineconversion.com or www.convert-me.com.

Recording their ideas

- Support children when drawing and completing the table, ensuring they write down the appropriate units.

- Once they have completed the table, encourage extension or support activities relating to measures. For example, collect various objects of different weights, lengths and capacities and provide imperial and metric measures for children to compare.

LANGUAGE ACTIVITY WORKSHEET

- This worksheet can be used to introduce or revise work on prepositions. Explain to the children that these words are used in sentences to show where people and things are, e.g. *under, across, above, on*. They can also be used to express time and cause, e.g. *before, after, during, since, because of*.

- Provide the children with the worksheet and point out the prepositions at the top of the sheet. Encourage the children to complete the sentences.

- Allow the children to share their work with others by reading out their own sentences and discussing the prepositions they used.

Answers: after, before, because of, during, since.

SPORTING PREPOSITIONS

Some prepositions give you information about
when things happen and why they happen.

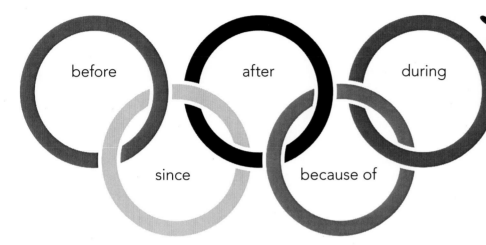

before   after   during

since   because of

Complete each of the sentences below.

Then underline the preposition used in each sentence.

After the runner jumped over the last hurdle,   _____

Before the swimmers dived into the pool,   _____

The high jumper could not take part because of   _____

The gold medal winner waved to the crowd during   _____

Tug of war has not been an Olympic sport since   _____

Write two of your own sentences using prepositions.

1. _____

2. _____

MOST LEAVES ON A CLOVER STEM

This gardening book page is about Shigeo Obara from Japan, who on 10 May 2009 broke the Guinness World Record for most leaves on a clover stem.

Text type:	recount
AFs covered:	AF2, AF3
Specialist vocabulary:	clover, leaf, leaves, rare, size, luck

ANSWERS

ON YOUR MARKS

a. People say that a four-leaf clover can bring you good luck. *Literal AF2*
b. Obara re-grew the clovers so he could have more rare clovers in his garden. *Inference AF3*
c. *Personal opinion AF3*

GET SET

a. A clover plant can be green or purple. *Literal AF2*
b. Obara mixed the clovers so that he could grow more unusual clovers. *Inference AF3*
c. Obara's 56-leaf clover brought him good luck: a Guinness World Record and fame as a clover grower. *Deduction AF3*

GO FOR GOLD!

a. In 1951, Obara found a few rare four-leaf clovers. *Literal AF2*
b. Obara loves growing clovers because he has been growing and caring for them in his garden for a long time. *Inference AF3*
c. Obara stuck number tabs on each clover leaf because they all looked alike, so he needed a way to remember which leaves he had counted. *Deduction AF3*

BEYOND THE RECORD

Shigeo Obara kept notes about all his clovers to help him grow different types and sizes. Choose a plant that you can find outside. How will you capture information about this plant and how will you share this information with your friends?

Background research, reading and discussion to help the children to prepare

- Collect flower/plant reference books and allow children access to websites such as www.flowers.org.uk/. Talk about the information provided for each plant, e.g. recognisable features, where it grows and its life cycle. Are labelled diagrams used? Why are these useful?
- Choose an area outside where the children can study plants in a safe environment. Remind the children beforehand that they should not pick wild flowers or plants.

Recording their ideas

- How will the children record their plant information? Will they use a camera, make notes and sketches, record sound files?
- How will they present their findings: as a poster, a page from a plant book? Will everything be handwritten or will they use a computer?
- Encourage the children to discuss their plants and findings with others in the class. Discuss why it is useful to keep notes on plants throughout the year, and how this helps gardeners and naturalists.

LANGUAGE ACTIVITY WORKSHEET

- This worksheet can be used to revise or introduce work on collective nouns. Point out the definition of a collective noun at the top of the worksheet. Look at the three examples: *a pride of lions, a choir of singers, a bunch of clover*. Encourage the children to think of a few more examples such as *a flock of sheep* or *a pack of wolves*. Ask the children to focus on the worksheet. Point out the need to think visually if they are not sure of the collective noun, e.g. *a row of houses*.
- Once they have completed the worksheet, give the children the resources to investigate other collective nouns and create a word bank. Discuss how some things can have more than one collective noun e.g. *a bunch/bouquet of flowers*.

Answers: team, herd, gaggle, swarm, pack, row, clump, bouquet.

COLLECTING COLLECTIVE NOUNS

A collective noun is a name used for a group of people, animals or objects.

A pride of lions   *A choir of singers*   *A bunch of clover*

Write the correct words from the two four-leaf clovers into the missing spaces to complete the collective nouns.

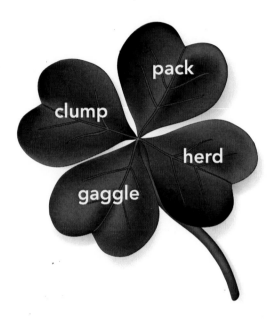

1. A _____ of footballers

2. A _____ of cows

3. A _____ of geese

4. A _____ of bees

5. A _____ of cards

6. A _____ of houses

7. A _____ of seaweed

8. A _____ of flowers

Find more collective nouns and create a word bank.

FARTHEST EAR SLING-SHOT

This explanation text, set as a page from a magazine supplement aimed at children, is about Monte Pierce, who broke the Guinness World Record for the farthest ear sling-shot.

Text type:	explanation/recount
AFs covered:	AF2, AF3, AF4, AF5
Specialist vocabulary:	earlobe, sling-shot, dangly, stretch, audience, farthest

ANSWERS

ON YOUR MARKS

a. **The earlobe is the soft part of the ear.** *Literal AF2*
b. **Monte used a small coin so it could fit onto his earlobe and because it was light.** *Inference AF3*
c. **Monte's nickname is 'Sling-back ears' because he can use his ears as sling-shots.** *Deduction AF3*

GET SET

a. **Monte Pierce broke the world record for the farthest ear sling-shot.** *Literal AF2*
b. **The word 'dangly' means hanging loosely.** *Inference AF5*
c. **A large measuring mat was needed because the coin was going to travel a long way.** *Deduction AF3*

GO FOR GOLD!

a. **The three adjectives are stretchy, long and dangly.** *Literal AF2, AF5*
b. **The third paragraph recounts what happened on the show.** *Deduction AF3, AF4*
c. *Personal opinion AF3*

BEYOND THE RECORD

Imagine you were interviewing Monte on *Lo Show dei Record*. What questions do you think the viewers would like to ask? Make a list of five questions you would ask.

Background research, reading and discussion to help the children to prepare

• Read through the comprehension text with the class (you may wish to ask some of the children to read out a sentence/paragraph).

• Ask the children to imagine they are a member of the audience, sitting in the television studio, watching the record attempt. What questions would they like to ask Monte Pierce? Give the children a few minutes to discuss in small groups and then report back.

Recording their ideas

• Explain to the children that they can write down as many questions as they like before they choose the best five.

• If children are working in groups, how will they choose the final five questions? Through discussion with others? By voting?

• Encourage the children to share their questions with others. Are the questions open (to elicit longer responses) or closed (only *yes* or *no* answers)? Are they repetitive? Which questions are the best? Why?

Ideas for questions may include: How nervous did you feel? Did the audience put you off? Did you train beforehand? How does it feel to be a Guinness World Record holder?

LANGUAGE ACTIVITY WORKSHEET

• Use the worksheet to introduce the determiners *a* and *an*. Briefly revise the terms *consonants* and *vowels*. Highlight 'an elastic band' in the comprehension text and underline the *an*. Ask the children whether the first letter of 'elastic' is a vowel or consonant. Explain the *a* and *an* rules with the children, using more examples. Explain that the words beginning with *u*, but with the sound *you*, do not use *an*.

• Point to the rules at the top of the worksheet. The activity allows the children to choose which determiner to use in a nonsense poem and then gives them the opportunity to write their own poem using *a* and *an* words. There is space for children to add more vowel words to the word bank at the bottom of the sheet for use in this activity and future work.

Answers: an, a, an, a, a.

**OFFICIALLY
AMAZING**

NONSENSE POEM

Use *a* in front of nouns and adjectives that begin with a consonant.
Use *an* in front of nouns and adjectives that begin with a vowel.

Write *a* or *an* in the gaps to finish the nonsense poem.

Today was _____ eventful day.

I met _____ young girl called Mae.

Her ear had _____ itch.

Then she fell in _____ ditch.

I hope tomorrow is _____ better day!

Write your own nonsense poem below using *a* and *an* words. Use the word bank at the bottom of the page for ideas.

Find some more *an* words to add to the word bank.

a	e	i	o	u – not 'you' – sounds
apple, actor, ant, aunt, amazing, aeroplane, airport, angry, alien, astronaut, alarm, axe	ear, early, elephant, empty, exam, explore, egg, engine	icy, igloo, idea, ill, inventor, itch, island	octopus, ocean, ogre, odd, old, orange, oven, ostrich	umbrella, ugly, underground, unkind, untidy, urn, upper, unhappy

FASTEST CROSSING OF THE SAHARA DESERT BY BICYCLE

This blog post is written about Reza Pakravan, who set the Guinness World Record for the fastest crossing of the Sahara Desert by bicycle.

Text type:	recount
AFs covered:	AF2, AF3
Specialist vocabulary:	desert, Sahara, tribe, bicycle, fastest, cycled

ANSWERS

ON YOUR MARKS

a. **Reza cycled across the Sahara Desert.** *Literal AF2*

b. **Reza drank 7 litres of water each day because he got thirsty from cycling through the hot desert.** *Deduction AF3*

c. **It would be hard to cycle in the desert because of the heat, sand, flies and no proper roads.** *Inference AF3*

GET SET

a. **It took Reza 13 days, 5 hours, 50 minutes, 14 seconds to cycle across the desert.** *Literal AF2*

b. **Reza was cycling to Sudan. He must have felt tired and very happy when he got there.** *Inference AF3*

c. **Evidence is information that shows that something has been done or is true. Reza needed evidence to show Guinness World Records that he had set the record without cheating.** *Deduction AF3, AF5*

GO FOR GOLD!

a. **In the desert, Reza had problems with flies, flat tyres and sandstorms.** *Literal AF2*

b. **Reza kept going because he had the right equipment, was fit, had a GPS tracking device, camping equipment or places to stay, and food and drink.** *Inference AF3*

c. **Reza had to train for four months so that he was fit enough to cycle long distances and to get used to the heat.** *Deduction AF3*

BEYOND THE RECORD

Search the internet for a film of Reza crossing the desert. Then write a travel blog imagining you are cycling in the Sahara Desert. A sandstorm is heading your way. Describe the storm and how you feel.

Background research, reading and discussion to help the children to prepare

• Guide children to websites with video of Reza's trip, e.g. www.cyclingsahara.com/about.htm (see MEDIA section).

• As a class, explore accounts of sandstorms in print and online: http://library.thinkquest.org/03oct/01027/sandstorm.html; www.environmentalgraffiti.com/featured/sandstorms-on-earth/2353. Discuss their effects and list words that could be used to describe them.

• Select examples of online travel blogs: www.telegraph.co.uk/travel/3391028/The-worlds-best-travel-blogs.html. Discuss their uses and features: like a diary, informal language, descriptive words, interesting, exciting, lots of detail, not too long.

Recording their ideas

• How will they record descriptive words and ideas from the images and information about sandstorms: a word bank, descriptive phrases or thoughts on paper or on computer?

• How will children write their blog: handwritten on paper, using a word-processing tool, directly into a school/class blog?

Ideas may include: sand in hair, nose, eyes; not being able to see or breathe properly; terror or very nervous; solid wall of sand. Include words relating to high speed, heat, sand rubbing, etc.

LANGUAGE ACTIVITY WORKSHEET

• This worksheet reinforces the use of time and cause conjunctions as a means to join up two simple single-clause sentences into a longer two-clause sentence.

• Guide the children to the examples at the top of the worksheet. Point out the conjunction and how there is only one starting capital letter and one full stop. Discuss how the conjunction sentence flows and reads better. Emphasise how the conjunctions are connected to time and give the reasons why someone or something does something.

• The children should read out their sentences to see if they make sense with the conjunctions. Point out how some sentences could have more than one conjunction but it changes the meaning of the sentence.

Answers: because, after, before, until, when, so, while.

COMBINING WITH CONJUNCTIONS

A conjunction is a word that can join two short-clause sentences into one sentence.
Declan zoomed along the zip wire. He landed in the sandpit.
Declan zoomed along the zip wire until he landed in the sandpit.

Complete the sentences below by adding in the correct conjunction words.
You should only use each conjunction once.

Make sure each sentence makes sense.

when   before   after   while   because   so   until

1. Meena does not like sailing _____ she gets seasick.

2. Ava and her brother went on a camel ride _____ they had breakfast.

3. The Carter family quickly set up their tent _____ it started to rain.

4. I am not going home _____ I have built my sandcastle.

5. Lou was cycling along the road _____ she suddenly saw a sandstorm coming towards her.

6. Harry wanted to go scuba diving _____ he could see the colourful fish and coral.

7. We are going pony trekking _____ Mum and Dad visit the ruined castle.

Use conjunctions to complete your own sentences.

1. We had an awful time at the theme park _____

2. There was a great barbecue on the beach _____

LONGEST JOURNEY BY POWERED PARAGLIDER

This adventure book text is about Benjamin Jordan, a Canadian photographer who broke the Guinness World Record for the longest journey by powered paraglider.

Text type:	recount
AFs covered:	AF2, AF3, AF5, AF6
Specialist vocabulary:	paraglider, Canada, photographer, journey, above, beyond

ANSWERS

ON YOUR MARKS

a. Benjamin Jordan is a photographer. *Literal AF2*

b. He used a powered paraglider because he wanted to travel a long way in a record time. *Inference AF3*

c. *Personal opinion AF6*

GET SET

a. Benjamin Jordan broke the world record for the longest journey by powered paraglider. *Literal AF2*

b. Benjamin would be a good person to talk to about following dreams because he has followed his dreams to break a world record, help others and do his photography. *Inference AF3*

c. The book was called *Above and Beyond* because it is about Benjamin's journey in the sky as well as about him achieving his dream. *Deduction AF3, AF5*

GO FOR GOLD!

a. Benjamin visited 50 youth camps and schools. *Literal AF2*

b. The children wrote 'Don't quit' to encourage Benjamin to continue his long journey and keep following his dream. *Inference AF3*

c. The journey may have encouraged some children to try and follow their dreams. It allowed some children from low-income families to have the chance to go to summer camp. *Deduction AF3*

BEYOND THE RECORD

Think of ways you could raise money for a good cause or charity by trying to break or set a Guinness World Record. Use a Mind Map™ to record your ideas. What would you do? Where? How? When? Who would be involved? Present your ideas on a poster to show to the class.

Background research, reading and discussion to help the children to prepare

- Guide children to online information from various charity groups on fund-raising ideas: www.fundraising-ideas.org/DIY/UKCollection.htm; www.gopak.co.uk/free-fundraising-ideas-guide/; www.macmillan.org.uk/Fundraising/FundraisingIdeas/FundraisingIdeas.aspx.

- Provide children with a copy of the Guinness World Records book or access to the website: www.guinnessworldrecords.com/.

- With the children, discuss why it is important to plan a fund-raising event before it takes place. How can working in teams help in organising it effectively? What types of records would be good to try and break, and which wouldn't?

Recording their ideas

- How will they choose their record? Decide on what is possible first, then choose a record? Decide on a record type first, then research? Browse through records until they see one they would like to try?

- What features will children include on their poster? Will they use drawings and sub-headings?

Ideas may include: venues, publicity (such as posters, tickets, sponsorship forms, contacting Guinness World Records to make it a proper record attempt), equipment needed.

LANGUAGE ACTIVITY WORKSHEET

- Use the worksheet to look at proper nouns. Revise any work done on common nouns and proper nouns, giving some examples.

- Emphasise how all proper nouns start with a capital letter. Discuss how proper nouns are names of people, places, days of the week, months, shops, brand names, etc.

- After the activity, discuss with the children which proper nouns and common nouns they put in their word bank. Ask some of the children to read through the sentences they have created.

Answers: month of the year, day of the week, place, place, person's name.

PARAGLIDING PROPER NOUNS

Proper nouns are names of people, places, days of the week and months.
They always start with a capital letter.

Look at the proper nouns below. Underneath each one, write down why it is a proper noun.

August

Monday

British Columbia

_____   _____   _____

Canada

Benjamin

_____   _____

Make a word bank of proper nouns and common nouns.
On a separate piece of paper, use some of the nouns to make sentences.

Proper nouns	Common nouns

LARGEST COLLECTION OF POOH AND FRIENDS MEMORABILIA

This magazine article is about Deb Hoffmann from Wisconsin, USA, who holds the Guinness World Record for the largest collection of Pooh and Friends memorabilia.

Text type:	recount
AFs covered:	AF2, AF3, AF5
Specialist vocabulary:	memorabilia, collection, object, largest, jam-packed, trawled

ANSWERS

ON YOUR MARKS

a. Deb Hoffmann lives near Waukesha in Wisconsin, USA. *Literal AF2*

b. She may need another room as she will eventually run out of space for her new Pooh objects. *Inference AF3*

c. *Personal opinion AF3*

GET SET

a. Deb Hoffmann started her collection when she fell in love with a Pooh phone. *Literal AF2*

b. The sunset would make the room 'glow yellow' because of the yellow colour of the Pooh objects. *Inference AF3, AF5*

c. 'Trawled' means searching or hunting for something. *Deduction AF3, AF5*

GO FOR GOLD!

a. The adjective 'jam-packed' suggests that the room is very full. *Literal AF2, AF5*

b. Deb wants more Pooh and Friends memorabilia because she enjoys looking for them and wants as many as possible. *Inference AF3*

c. She means that she loves the excitement of looking for something and then finding it. *Deduction AF3, AF5*

BEYOND THE RECORD

Do you have a collection? How would you present this to friends? If you don't collect anything, what would you like to collect and how would you start your collection?

Background research, reading and discussion to help the children to prepare

• As a class, search online for images of collections. Use these images to stimulate discussion on what children might like to collect themselves.

• Talk about why people collect things and how they collect them, care for them and display them.

• Allow children access to online information about the subject of collecting things, e.g. www.42explore.com/collect2.htm; www.24hourmuseum.org.uk/downloads/mclass.pdf.

Recording their ideas

• How will children present their collection? As a script to be read out, a Microsoft PowerPoint® presentation with images, a display with labels and information captions?

• For those children who are choosing a collection, how will they decide on what they would like to collect? Will their choice be linked to an interest, or will they use the internet to gather ideas? Can they give good reasons for their choice? How will they record their plans, e.g. a Mind Map™, written notes in a logical order?

LANGUAGE ACTIVITY WORKSHEET

• Use this worksheet to reinforce the idea of grouping information into paragraphs. Remind the children that paragraphs can be used to group similar information together. Hand out the worksheet and point to the sticky notes. Show the children the writer's paragraph plan and discuss how it can help to organise her notes efficiently.

• Once the children have completed the worksheet, encourage them to discuss why they chose the information in each paragraph and how the sentences are linked together. Emphasise how paragraphs help the reader, as they break up writing into clear and easy-to-understand sections.

Answers: h, b, c; j, i; e, g; k, d; a, f.

SORTING OUT WINNIE

A writer needs to sort these notes into the correct sections of her paragraph plan. Can you help her?

Write down the best order for the sentences in the table below. The first one has been done for you.

Winnie-the-Pooh and Christopher Robin

a) Christopher Robin's dad wrote stories about the toys for him.

b) Harry found a bear cub with no parents.

c) Harry called the bear 'Winnipeg' or 'Winnie' for short.

d) Christopher Robin's other toys were a donkey, a piglet, a tiger and a kangaroo and her baby.

e) Many people came to see Winnie the bear.

f) The stories became world famous.

g) A young boy called Christopher Robin liked to visit Winnie.

h) Harry Colebourn was a Canadian soldier in World War I.

i) Winnie lived in London Zoo until she died in 1934.

j) Harry took Winnie to Britain.

k) Christopher Robin called his teddy bear 'Winnie'.

Paragraph sections	Information
Who was Harry Colebourn and who did he find?	1. h
	2.
	3.
Where did Winnie live?	1.
	2.
Who came to see Winnie?	1.
	2.
Who were Christopher Robin's toys?	1.
	2.
Who wrote *Winnie the Pooh*?	1.
	2.

LARGEST MUSEUM DEVOTED TO DINOSAURS

This leaflet-style text for museum visitors provides information about the Shandong Tianyu Museum of Nature in China, which holds the Guinness World Record for the largest museum devoted to dinosaurs.

Text type:	persuasion
AFs covered:	AF2, AF3, AF5
Specialist vocabulary:	dinosaur, museum, fossil, prehistoric, fauna, skeleton

ANSWERS

ON YOUR MARKS

a. The name of the museum is the Shandong Tianyu Museum of Nature. *Literal AF2*

b. Two verbs that mean 'to walk' are wander and stroll. *Deduction AF2, AF5*

c *Personal opinion AF3*

GET SET

a. The museum is devoted to dinosaurs and prehistoric fauna. *Literal AF2*

b. 'Dinosaur objects' could be the bones, teeth and eggs of dinosaurs. *Inference AF3, AF5*

c. You would marvel because it would be amazing to see a fossil of something so very small and old. *Inference AF3, AF5*

GO FOR GOLD!

a. The museum is 'a place you will never forget' because of its (list of possible reasons): large number of dinosaur objects; amazing dinosaur displays; magical halls of stones; thousands of fossils; 4D cinema. *Literal AF2, AF5*

b. 'Prehistoric fauna' means animals that lived a long time ago. *Deduction AF3, AF5*

c. *Personal opinion AF2, AF3*

BEYOND THE RECORD

Use the internet to find out more about Shandong Tianyu Museum of Nature. How would you persuade somebody to visit?

Background research, reading and discussion to help the children to prepare

• Guide children to the Shandong Tianyu Museum website: www.tynhm.com/ (the website will need to be translated into English).

• As a class, visit the Guinness World Records website at www.guinnessworldrecords.com/ to find out about other records the museum holds (largest turquoise, largest scheelite crystal, largest amethyst geode, largest Sinosauropteryx fossil, longest tree trunk fossil – silicified).

• Use the comprehension text to discuss the features of persuasive writing. Discuss how the text makes the reader want to visit the museum. Use a highlighter for the features – emotive language, descriptive language, introduction and conclusion, and use of the present tense.

Recording their ideas

• How will the children sequence the information they find? Do they need dictionaries and thesauruses to help with their vocabulary?

• How will the information be presented: handwritten or printed? In a leaflet, a poster or as a Microsoft PowerPoint® presentation? Will it include pictures or photographs?

Ideas may include: facilities at the museum, descriptive words for a hall or object, emotive language for different aspects of the museum, facts and figures, bulleted lists, captions.

LANGUAGE ACTIVITY WORKSHEET

• This worksheet encourages the children to use sub-headings as an aid to their presentations and as a way of finding what they need from a piece of information. If possible, show a piece of work that includes sub-headings and headings. Discuss why they are useful for presentations.

• Once they have completed the activity, discuss why the sub-headings make the information easier to read. Play a game in which the children have to find a specific piece of information from the text. How did the sub-headings help them locate it?

Answers: Possible sub-headings are What are fossils?, How are fossils made?, Where are fossils found?, How can I find fossils?

FOSSIL SUB-HEADINGS

The sub-headings for the fossil information below are missing. Read each section and write a sub-heading for each one.

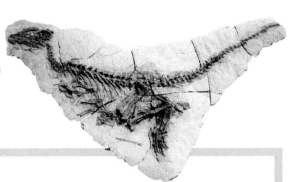

FOSSILS

_____

Fossils are parts of dead prehistoric plants or animals that, over millions of years, have left impressions or shapes in rock. Studying fossils can help us see what the creatures and plants might have looked like.

_____

A fossil is made when a creature dies and is buried in mud, sand or small stones. As more is layered on top of the creature, its flesh rots leaving hard bones. Over time, the layers turn into hard rock and the bones begin to disappear. As they do, the minerals in the rock fill in the bone shapes, making an impression in the rock.

_____

Fossils can be found all over the world where there is sedimentary rock, such as the cliffs at Lyme Regis in Dorset and rocks at Brora in Scotland. Most are not easy to find and need to be dug up.

_____

For fossil hunting you need a hammer, chisel, a pair of safety glasses, a strong bag and hammering gloves. To be safe, it is best to go fossil hunting with an adult.

MOST STEPS CLIMBED BY BICYCLE

This magazine-style text is about Zhang Jincheng from China, Xavi Casas from Andorra and Javier Zapata from Colombia, who broke the Guinness World Record for the most steps climbed by bicycle.

Text type:	non-chronological report/recount
AFs covered:	AF2, AF3, AF5, AF6
Specialist vocabulary:	stair, climb, building, extreme, bounce, tower

ANSWERS

ON YOUR MARKS

a. **Jin Mao Tower is in Shanghai, China.** *Literal AF2*

b. *Personal opinion AF3*

c. **The cyclists chose the Jin Mao Tower because it is very high and hard to cycle up.** *Inference AF3*

GET SET

a. **Stair climbing is a 'difficult skill' because the cyclists have to stand up on their bikes and bounce from step to step without touching the ground, walls or any other part of the building.** *Literal AF2*

b. **The cyclists climbed 2,008 steps to mark the year of the Beijing Olympics in China – 2008.** *Inference AF3*

c. **The Chinese people wanted to give the cyclists a big party to celebrate the fact that they had achieved the world record.** *Deduction AF3*

GO FOR GOLD!

a. **The cyclists cycled up the tower to set the Guinness World Record and to welcome in 2008, the year of the Beijing Olympics.** *Literal AF2*

b. **'Extreme cyclists' are cyclists who cycle in very difficult or dangerous places.** *Inference AF3, AF5*

c. **It would be hard for the cyclists not to touch the ground, walls or any other part of the building as they may need to hold on to something if they lose balance or go round corners.** *Deduction AF3*

BEYOND THE RECORD

Find out more about the extreme sport of stair climbing by bicycle. Two of the cyclists have other records for stair climbing. What makes them want to do it? How do they train? What kind of bikes do they use?

Background research, reading and discussion to help the children to prepare

• Guide children to websites such as http://english.cri. cn/3100/2008/01/01/1261@309955.htm. A film of the successful record attempt can also be found at www.youtube.com/ watch?v=6-PCkASC7v8. You may wish to bookmark other relevant websites for use in class.

• Talk about the film of the record attempt. Discuss how the children would feel if they were one of the athletes.

• Children can use the Guinness World Records site to search for the three record holders and other records they hold (type directly in the 'Search records' box): see www.guinnessworldrecords.com.

Recording their ideas

• Encourage the children to record their initial ideas. This could be done as a simple list, sticky notes, a Mind Map™ or written notes under simple headings.

• How will they present their information? As a fact file, a Microsoft PowerPoint® presentation, an 'interview' with one of the athletes?

LANGUAGE ACTIVITY WORKSHEET

• Use this worksheet to revise or introduce prefixes. Discuss how some root words can have prefixes and suffixes added to them, e.g. *port* (meaning *to carry*): *import, export, porter, portable.*

• This worksheet looks at the root word *cycle* and shows how other spellings related to this word can be learned by adding various prefixes such as *bi, tri, uni, motor* and *re*. Allow the children access to dictionaries or word banks if they need help in matching the correct definitions to the words.

• Once they have completed the worksheet, discuss how learning the prefixes for the different meanings of *cycle* can help the children spell the words correctly.

Answers: Tricycle – a riding machine with three wheels that moves by pushing pedals; recycle – to re-use something; motorcycle – a riding machine with two wheels and an engine; unicycle – a riding machine with one wheel; bicycle – a riding machine with two wheels that moves by pushing pedals.

CYCLING WORDS

The word *cycle* is from the Greek for *wheel*.
It also means something that is repeated again and again.

Draw lines to match each definition to the correct word in the wheel.

bicycle

a riding machine with three wheels that moves
by pushing pedals

unicycle

to re-use something

tricycle

a riding machine with two wheels and an engine

motorcycle

a riding machine with one wheel

recycle

a riding machine with two wheels that moves
by pushing pedals

Use each of the words in a sentence.

1. _____

2. _____

3. _____

4. _____

5. _____

NOTES

Use this page to make notes about the reading comprehension texts and activities or any topic/subject links with your curriculum to share with other class teachers.